Introduction

"The good Lord didn't see fit to put oil and gas only where there are democratically elected regimes friendly to the United States. Occasionally we have to operate in places where, all things considered, one would not normally choose to go. But, we go where the business is."[1]
- Richard Cheney, 1998

"There is no instance of a country having benefited from prolonged warfare."[2]
- Sun Tzu, 512 b.c.

On January 17th 1961, in his final public speech as President of the United States, Dwight Eisenhower expressed his fear that the relationship between legislators, national armed forces and industrial sectors could begin to endanger liberties and democratic process. He termed this the 'military-industrial complex'.[3] Dan Briody uses the analogy of an 'iron triangle' to describe this alliance, in which "the world's mightiest military intersects with high-powered politics and big business."[4] This relationship dictates policy-making, corrupting a government into preventing or ignoring the actual needs of the citizenry it is meant to represent, in favour of special interests. This study will examine this concept in relation to the United States' foreign policy regarding Iraq under the presidency of George W. Bush.

i. Background to the Iraq War

On September 20th 2001, following the hijacking of commercial airliners and coordinated suicide attacks in the largest terrorist attack on United States territory; President George W. Bush launched the War on Terror. This military campaign called for the invasion and intervention in nations around the world, from the Philippines to Somalia, with the stated objective of defeating the "radical network of terrorists and every government that supports them."[5] Amongst the conflicts launched was the most privatised war in the world's history, waged against a nation which had never threatened nor been implicated in any attack against United States territory,[6] the 2003 Iraq War, otherwise known as Operation Iraqi Freedom.

On January 28th 2003 President George W. Bush gave the State of Union Address justifying the invasion of Iraq. He claimed that President of Iraq, Saddam Hussein, had links to terrorist

---

[1] Cheney, R. (1998). *Defending Liberty in a Global Economy*. Available: http://www.cato.org/speeches/sp-dc062398.html. Last accessed 30th May 2011.
[2] Sun Tzu (2010). *The Art of War*. London: Arcturus Publishing Limited. Pg. 22
[3] Eisenhower, D. (2011). *Farewell Address January 17, 1961*. Available: http://www.eisenhowermemorial.org/pages.php?pid=696. Last accessed 30th May 2011.
[4] Briody, D (2004). *The Iron Triangle*. New Jersey: John Wiley & Sons. Pg. xxvi
[5] The Washington Post. (2003). *Text of President Bush's 2003 State of the Union Address*. Available: http://www.washingtonpost.com/wp-srv/onpolitics/transcripts/bushtext_012803.html. Last accessed 6th Nov 2011.
[6] Zunes, S. 'An Annotated Overview of the Foreign Policy Segments of President George W. Bush's State of the Union Address,' *Foreign Policy in Focus*, January 29, 2003.

1

organisations and possessed chemical weapons, which threatened the security of the United States.[7] He delivered a black and white portrayal of global politics, referring to an undefined 'terrorist' enemy, a group whose goals are the relentless pursuit of destruction and death based on a perverse strand of Islam. Exceptional force was justified as the only way to counter their actions. George W. Bush claimed: "Saddam Hussein aids and protects terrorists, including members of al-Qaeda."[8] Former White House Counsel John Dean argued that during his speech "Bush presented so many distorted beliefs, estimates, guesstimates, that it appears he was misleading the public and the congress."[9] The Bush administration provided over thirty reasons to invade and occupy Iraq,[10] including claims later to be proven false that Saddam Hussein operated a nuclear program and was involved with al-Qaeda.[11] [12] United States Deputy Secretary of Defence, Paul Wolfowitz, claimed that Iraq's 'possession of weapons of mass destruction' was the US government's 'core reason' for the invasion.[13] Nearly two years after the invasion of Iraq, Charles Duelfer, leader of the investigative Iraq Survey Group, reported that the search for weapons of mass destruction had been given up and that no stockpiles of weapons had existed in Iraq when Coalition forces invaded.[14] John Prados argues, "the Bush administration justification for war comes down to stockpiles of Saddam's weapons of mass destruction. Reveal those stocks to have been mythical, and nothing remains."[15] In hindsight we now know the evidence cited as justification for the decision to go to war was based on poor intelligence.

A key member of the media supporting a call for the Iraq War was Judith Miller, former journalist at *The New York Times*. Much of Miller's reporting pertaining to Saddam Hussein's possession of lethal weapons came from 'leaked' information which later transpired was based upon false evidence or entirely fabricated.[16] The myths surrounding Iraq's possession of nuclear, biological or chemical weapons were bolstered as the Bush administration cited Miller's

---

[7] The Washington Post. (2003). *Text of President Bush's 2003 State of the Union Address*. Available: http://www.washingtonpost.com/wp-srv/onpolitics/transcripts/bushtext_012803.html. Last accessed 6th Nov 2011.
[8] *Ibid.*
[9] Dean, J. *Uncovered: The War on Iraq*, 2004. [DVD] Robert Greenwald, USA: Cinema Libre Studio.
[10] Kick, R (2004). *50 Things You're Not Supposed to Know: Volume 2*. New York: The Disinformation Company Ltd. Pg. 86
[11] Ivins, M; Dubose, L (2004). *Bushwhacked*. London: Allison & Busby Limited. Pg. 268
[12] Polk, W (2005). *Understanding Iraq*. London: I.B.Tauris & Co Ltd. Pg. 200
[13] United States Department of Defense. (2003). *Deputy Secretary Wolfowitz Interview with Sam Tannenhaus, Vanity Fair*. Available: http://www.defense.gov/transcripts/transcript.aspx?transcriptid=2594. Last accessed 16th Nov 2011.
[14] BBC News. (2005). *US Gives Up Search for Iraq WMD*. Available: http://news.bbc.co.uk/1/hi/world/americas/4169107.stm. Last accessed 22nd Oct 2011.
[15] Prados, J (2004). *Hoodwinked*. New York: The New Press. Pg. 355
[16] Ricks, T (2007). *Fiasco*. London: Penguin Group. Pg. 35

reporting as evidence to support their own claims.[17] Noam Chomsky characterises this mechanism as the 'manufacturing of fear'.[18] Iraqi citizen Rafid al-Janabi who defected from Iraq in 1999, informed the Central Intelligence Agency that he had been a chemical engineer at a plant which produced mobile weapons laboratories as part of Iraq's weapons of mass destruction program.[19] This information was a key element of the rationale for military action in Iraq in 2003. It was only in February of 2011 that al-Janabi admitted to *The Guardian* newspaper that he had fabricated his claims "in an attempt to bring down the Saddam Hussein regime."[20] CIA senior official Tyler Drumheller spoke of al-Janabi as "a guy trying to get his green card essentially… and playing the system for what it was worth."[21] We can understand the invasion of Iraq as the result of those in command demanding evidence that could link Saddam Hussein with al-Qaeda and the perpetrators of the September 11th attacks. They used those seeking personal gain with false evidence, to build a dossier for war.

ii. Business and the Iraq War

On March 20th 2003 the invasion of Iraq began with long-range Tomahawk missiles striking buildings in the capital Baghdad. Soon after, not only troops but tens of thousands of private contractors entered the country; providing everything from logistical support and construction to security and communications. The right of private companies to be involved in the war effort came eighteen years before with the establishment of a particular army regulation, the Logistics Civil Augmentation Program. A report published in 2009 by the Congressional Research Service estimated that by then there were nearly 133,000 private contractors in Iraq.[22] It admitted that research into the issue had only begun in 2007 and that reports from contractors had not been checked for accuracy. The profits these companies have amassed are astounding. The Congressional Budget Office released a report in 2008 which claimed that one in five dollars spent on the Iraq War went to private contractors and that up until 2007, $85 billion dollars worth of contracts had been awarded.[23] The void between what the Iraq War was

[17] Rossi, M (2009). *What Every American Should Know About Who's Really Running the World.* New York: Nation Books. Pg. 175

[18] Chomsky, N (2004). *Hegemony or Survival.* 3rd ed. London: Penguin Group. Pg. 121

[19] Drogin, B; Goetz, J. (2005). *How U.S. Fell Under the Spell of 'Curveball'.* Available: http://www.latimes.com/news/nationworld/iraq/complete/la-na-curveball20nov20,0,7743996.story. Last accessed 24th Oct 2011.

[20] Chulov, M; Pidd, H. (2011). *Defector Admits to WMD Lies That Triggered Iraq War.* Available: http://www.guardian.co.uk/world/2011/feb/15/defector-admits-wmd-lies-iraq-war. Last accessed 24th Oct 2011.

[21] BBC News. (2007). *Iraq War Source's Name Revealed.* Available: http://news.bbc.co.uk/1/hi/world/middle_east/7075501.stm. Last accessed 24th Oct 2011.

[22] Congressional Research Service. (2009). *Department of Defense Contractors in Iraq and Afghanistan: Background and Analysis.* Available: fpc.state.gov/documents/organization/128824.pdf. Last accessed 12th Dec 2011.

[23] Risen, J. (2008). *Use of Iraq Contractors Costs Billions, Report Says.* Available:

outlined to be and what it has become raises many questions about the intentions of those who started and orchestrated the conflict. What role did business interests have to play in deciding Iraq's future, was there legislation in place to prevent corporate exploitation and did the relationship between government and private contractors create a perpetual profit-driven conflict that will see an ever-lasting American presence in Iraq?

Six months after the US-led invasion, angered Iraqi citizens were joining violent insurgency groups. "They felt dishonoured by the presence of foreign troops on Iraqi soil… they blamed the Americans for the lack of security, jobs, and electricity."[24] Growing disillusion with the occupying forces saw escalating violence over the years. In October 2006 over one hundred US soldiers were killed, with an average of one hundred and eighty attacks every day.[25] As of January 2012 the war has cost the lives of over 4,800 members of the Iraq Coalition forces,[26] almost 4,500 of them soldiers from the United States military. At least 104,000 civilians have lost their lives to the conflict[27] with evidence to suggest that the deaths of many thousands more have been missed or deliberately excluded from official reports. The other cost of the war has been financial. The Congressional Research Service estimated that by the end of fiscal year 2011 the total war funding for Iraq would be $806 billion.[28] Back in 2006 the Iraq Study Group Report estimated the final cost of the U.S. involvement in Iraq would reach $2 trillion.[29] An investigation by Joseph Stiglitz and Linda Blimes in 2008, estimated the true cost of the Iraq War at $3 trillion. They claim that this figure "in all likelihood errs on the low side."[30] The exact cost of the war is extremely difficult to calculate. Much of the data is imprecise and knowing where the costs of a war 'end' is open to interpretation.

The War on Terror has given "a shot in the arm to the international arms trade."[31] Global military spending increased by 45% between 1998 and 2007, with 30% of that increase coming after 2001.[32] The pressure for the United States to go to war has, in part, come from lobbying of

http://www.nytimes.com/2008/08/12/washington/12contractors.html. Last accessed 24th Oct 2011.

[24] Chandrasekaran, R (2008). *Imperial Life in the Emerald City*. London: Bloomsbury Publishing Plc. Pg. 209

[25] Baker, J; Hamilton, L (2006). *The Iraq Study Group Report*. New York: Vintage Books. Pg. 3

[26] Iraq Coalition Casualty Count. (2012). *Operation Iraqi Freedom*. Available: http://icasualties.org/Iraq/index.aspx. Last accessed 1st Jan 2012.

[27] Iraq Body Count. (2012). *Documented Civilian Deaths from Violence*. Available: http://www.iraqbodycount.org/. Last accessed 1st Jan 2012.

[28] Belasco, A. (2011). *The Cost of Iraq, Afghanistan, and Other Global War on Terror Operations Since 9/11*. Available: www.fas.org/sgp/crs/natsec/RL33110.pdf. Last accessed 4th Jan 2012. Pg. 1

[29] Baker, J; Hamilton, L (2006). *The Iraq Study Group Report*. New York: Vintage Books. Pg. 32

[30] Stiglitz, J; Bilmes, L (2008). *The Three Trillion Dollar War*. London: Penguin Group. Pg. 31

[31] Gilby, N (2009). *The No-Nonsense Guide to the Arms Trade*. 2nd ed. Oxford: New Internationalist Publications Ltd. Pg. 25

[32] *Ibid.*

the government by profit-driven interest groups. Gore Vidal describes the Bush administration as being headed by "the oil-and-gas Cheney-Bush junta,"[33] a group that received nearly $2 million from the oil and gas industry in the year 2000.[34] The Republican Party under George W. Bush received millions in campaign contributions from individuals and private organisations prior to taking command. According to CorpWatch, a non-profit investigative research group, in 2004, when George W. Bush was re-elected, the aerospace, defence and security technology company Lockheed Martin contributed over $2 million towards his U.S. Presidential election campaign.[35] It would soon go on to profit from the war. Between 1989 and 2011 the company donated nearly $21 million in campaign contributions, split evenly between both the Democratic and Republican political parties.[36] They have been rewarded well. Since 1996 they have become the number one recipient of Pentagon outsourcing. The company has been awarded over $94 billion in government contracts and in 2006 held ten percent of all government contracts issued, not only those related to the military. This far exceeds the amount given to any other single contractor.[37] Not only Lockheed Martin, but a close-circle of inter-related businesses, with ties to government officials and members, with the power to command warfare, have benefitted from the Iraq War. Investment firms such as The Carlyle Group received huge revenues from defence spending, while being well connected to the Bush family and their associates. During the invasions of both Afghanistan and Iraq they employed the President's father, George H. W. Bush[38] and received investment from the wealthy bin Laden family.[39] In the same year the United States invaded Iraq, the group was managing $16.2 billion worth of funds, the vast majority of which was invested in businesses like multinational defence company BAE Systems and weapons manufacturer United Defense. This made Carlyle the eleventh-largest defence contractor in the United States.[40] Dan Briody describes The Carlyle Group as a key example of 'cronyism': "Over time, the pattern of Carlyle's hiring practices emerges to reveal a series of old friends helping one another out."[41]

---

[33] Vidal, G (2003). *Dreaming War*. Wiltshire: Cromwell Press Limited. Pg. 12
[34] Juhasz, A (2006). *The Bush Agenda*. New York: HarperCollins Publishers Inc. Pg. 6
[35] CorpWatch. (2011). *Lockheed Martin*. Available: http://www.corpwatch.org/section.php?id=9. Last accessed 13th Oct 2011.
[36] The Center for Responsive Politics. (2011). *Top All-Time Donors, 1989-2012*. Available: http://www.opensecrets.org/orgs/list.php. Last accessed 13th Oct 2011.
[37] Rossi, M (2009). *What Every American Should Know About Who's Really Running the World*. New York: Nation Books. Pg. 252
[38] Briody, D (2003). *The Iron Triangle*. New Jersey: John Wiley & Sons. Pg. 14
[39] Eichenwald, K (2001) 'Bin Laden Family Liquidates Holdings with Carlyle Group,' *New York Times*, October 26th 2001.
[40] Berman, P (2003) 'Lucky Twice,' *Forbes*, December 8th 2003.
[41] Briody, D (2003). *The Iron Triangle*. New Jersey: John Wiley & Sons. Pg. 22

A key example of the 'revolving door' politics, which took place under the Bush administration, was the conflicted interests of former Director of the Central Intelligence Agency, Robert Woolsey. Whilst serving as an advisor to Secretary of Defense Donald Rumsfeld and employed as a member of a number of institutions that advocated the invasion of Iraq, including the Foundation for the Defense of Democracies, Woolsey was also a member on the boards of two companies that profited from the war, including private military contractor DynCorp International Inc.[42] The same month the United States invaded Iraq, he was a key speaker at a conference for consulting firm Booz Allen Hamilton Inc., and was paid thousands of dollars to outline business opportunities available in the country's reconstruction.[43] The former foreign policy specialist benefitted financially from the decisions made by the government he was influencing, abusing his role in government for personal gain. Non-governmental organisations such as the 'Committee for the Liberation of Iraq' launched successful lobbying campaigns that encouraged intervention in Iraq and the expansion of NATO alliances. The Chairman of that particular group was George Shultz, a politician who had been President and Director of the largest engineering company in the world, Bechtel Group.[44] The company went on to receive requests for proposals from the Bush administration a month before the 2003 invasion. They were then rewarded with a $680 million contract, which was later expanded, and then in 2004 received a second contract, bringing its total earnings to more than $2.8 billion.[45] A whole group of well-connected politicians have had their financial interests in the invasion of Iraq exposed. Former State Department advisor Neil Livingstone repeatedly used his position to advocate war whilst managing GlobalOptions Inc. a company that provided contacts and consultation to companies operating in Iraq.[46] Joe Allbaugh, manager of George W. Bush's presidential election campaign in 2000, capitalised on Bush's policy decisions by setting up New Bridge Strategies LLC and Diligence LLC after the invasion. Both companies assisted clients in taking advantage of business opportunities in Iraq.[47] These are not sporadic acts by rogue former government officials but strong indicators of the relationship between government and corporate interests. The opportunity to create a business that could immediately receive government contracts led civil servants within the state to quit their positions, become incorporated, and to bid on the

[42] Roche, W; Silverstein, K. (2004). *Advocates of War Now Profit From Iraq's Reconstruction.* Available: http://www.commondreams.org/headlines04/0714-01.htm. Last accessed 6th June 2011.
[43] *Ibid.*
[44] Rossi, M (2009). *What Every American Should Know About Who's Really Running the World.* New York: Nation Books. Pg. 277
[45] Juhasz, A (2006). *The Bush Agenda.* New York: HarperCollins Publishers Inc. Pg. 229-230
[46] Roche, W; Silverstein, K. (2004). *Advocates of War Now Profit From Iraq's Reconstruction.* Available: http://articles.latimes.com/2004/jul/14/nation/na-advocates14. Last accessed 1st Jan 2012.
[47] Edsall, T; Eilperin, J. (2003). *Lobbyists Set Sights On Money-Making Opportunities in Iraq.* Available: http://www.washingtonpost.com/ac2/wp-dyn/A30907-2003Oct1. Last accessed 6th Nov 2011.

contracts they once supervised.[48] Naomi Klein argues that the merging of business and government, with regard to Iraq, was so prevalent that "the effect has been to eliminate the so-called revolving door between government and industry and put in 'an archway.'"[49]

iii. Implications of the Iraq War

President George W. Bush announced on May 1st 2003 that "major combat operations in Iraq have ended. In the Battle of Iraq, the United States and our allies have prevailed."[50] In the following seven months, before the year finished, over four thousand more Iraqi civilians would be killed[51] along with over three hundred and sixty soldiers from the US and coalition forces.[52] With major combat efforts continuing to take place in the following eight years, it appears that the statements made to cameras and crew aboard the USS Lincoln were to boost public support for the war and allude to a victorious end, where in reality there was no end in sight.

The war ended for a second time on the 14th December 2011 when, at the United States Army installation of Fort Bragg in North Carolina, President Barack Obama claimed that as Commander-in-Chief of the United States Armed Forces he had ordered the last of the combat troops out of the region by the end of the year.[53] Four days later a convoy comprised of hundreds of vehicle, carrying thousands of US troops, crossed out of Iraq into Kuwait, many of the vehicles being driven by men from South Asia, hired by private contractors.[54] Despite an end to the US military occupation, Deputy National Security Advisor Denis McDonough admitted that a civilian military presence of between four and five thousand security contractors would remain in Iraq.[55] *The Washington Post* reported that sixteen thousand diplomats and private contractors would stay in the country following the official end to the war.[56]

Eight days after the official removal of United States military troops from Iraq, sectarian violence erupted in a series of car and roadside bombs in the capital Baghdad killing nearly

---

[48] Chatterjee, P (2009). *Halliburton's Army*. New York: Nation Books. Pg. 113

[49] Klein, N (2008). *The Shock Doctrine*. 2nd ed. London: Penguin Group. Pg. 316

[50] BBC News. (2003). *Bush Speech: Full Text*. Available: http://news.bbc.co.uk/1/hi/world/americas/2994345.stm. Last accessed 11 Nov 2011.

[51] Iraq Body Count. (2011). *Documented Civilian Deaths From Violence*. Available: http://www.iraqbodycount.org/database/. Last accessed 14th Oct 2011.

[52] Cable News Network. (2011). *Iraq and Afghanistan War Causalities*. Available: http://www.cnn.com/SPECIALS/war.casualties/index.html. Last accessed 14th Oct 2011.

[53] BBC News. (2011). *Transcript: President Obama Iraq Speech*. Available: http://www.bbc.co.uk/news/world-us-canada-16191394. Last accessed 15th Dec 2011.

[54] Carlstrom, G. (2011). *US Military Winds Down Iraq Withdrawal*. Available: http://www.aljazeera.com/news/middleeast/2011/12/201112717295310300.html. Last accessed 19 Dec 2011.

[55] Eddlem, T. (2011). *Obama Proclaims End of Iraq War as Contractor War Continues*. Available: http://thenewamerican.com/usnews/foreign-policy/9491-obama-proclaims-end-of-iraq-war-as-contractor-war-continues. Last accessed 12th Dec 2011.

[56] Wilson, S. (2011). *All U.S. Troops to Leave Iraq by The End of 2011*. Available: http://www.washingtonpost.com/world/national-security/all-us-troops-to-leave-iraq/2011/10/21/gIQAUyJi3L_story.html. Last accessed 3rd Dec 2011.

seventy people and wounding hundreds more.[57] Four days later a car bomb exploded at the gates of Iraq's interior ministry, killing at least seven people.[58] The violence has continued on into 2012. Pratap Chatterjee argues the reason that the military action in Iraq failed to meet its objectives of maintaining order, establishing government and rebuilding infrastructure was due to the 'fragility' of its initial plans. The policy of using thousands of expatriate private contractors for reconstruction after the initial invasion was predicated on payment that would come from Iraq's oil reserves. When the oil took longer to extract, refine and trade than planned, companies exploited the circumstances to maximise profits. The remedy was the introduction of private military and security companies to defend the 'terrified businessmen'. These companies exacerbated the situation because they were poorly trained and their role undefined. They created resentment and infuriation amongst the local population who were without employment and basic amenities.[59] This contributed to the rise of militias formed of disbanded soldiers, angered civilians and other combatants whose goal is to incite violence against the occupying forces and other groups, and to take control themselves.

In the following chapters this study examines the relationship between private contractors and government in the build-up, invasion and occupation of Iraq, tracing the consequences of the privatisation that occurred, from the bidding on the contracts to the results they created. Effectively legislative measures were put in place prior to the invasion, which insured that a select group of businesses could profit from services the military had traditionally provided. Without any budgetary constraints from the federal government there was no incentive for these corporations to insure maximum efficiency when completing contracts. The result of this was companies billing the government for inflated costs, works being left incomplete as contracts expired and those issuing the contracts, or subcontracting, becoming exposed to bribery as war profiteering became big business. Where companies failed to build the infrastructure to get Iraq functioning adequately the disillusioned turned to the insurgent groups within the country and began countering the US-led occupation with violence, perpetuating the war further. The corporate intervention in Iraq went deeper. Often members of government were shareholders in the very companies that were awarded these contracts, creating conflicts of interest that only lead to the ceaselessness Eisenhower warned was a threat to keeping the peace when describing the military-industrial complex. It now appears, nearly nine years after the initial invasion, that

---

[57] BBC News. (2011). *Baghdad Blasts*. Available: http://www.bbc.co.uk/news/world-middle-east-16311802. Last accessed 24th Dec 2011.
[58] BBC News. (2011). *Iraq Interior Ministry Hit by Suicide Car Bomber*. Available: http://www.bbc.co.uk/news/world-middle-east-16330865. Last accessed 27th Dec 2011.
[59] Chatterjee, P (2004). *Iraq, Inc.* Toronto: Seven Stories Press. Pg. 13

the war made a select few very wealthy at the expense of a nation and that there is still no end in sight for the corporate occupation of Iraq. President Barack Obama gave a speech on the 1ˢᵗ September 2010 claiming that Operation Iraqi Freedom was over and that Operation New Dawn was in effect, an operation in which the United States was taking the role of advising and assisting the Iraqi military but only engaging in combat if necessary.[60] Seven months later a report by the Congressional Research Service estimated that as of March that same year, there were approximately 64,253 Department of Defense contract personnel in Iraq, making up 58% of the overall workforce,[61] meaning there were more employees of private companies on the ground than military soldiers. It also found that between 2005 and 2010, $112.1 billion was spent on contracts in Iraq by the federal government. *The New York Times* reported that at its peak in 2008 contractors were employing at least 180,000 private personnel on the ground in Iraq.[62] Naomi Klein is correct when she describes Iraq as the 'corporatist state',[63] a new arena of exploitation and plunder that conflated business interests with national interests, a drive for profit at any cost, even if it worked against the stated objective of bringing democracy and liberal ideals to a rebuilt Iraq.

A wider question is also asked of the contracting that occurred during the war. Political economist Max Weber defines the State as "a corporate group that has compulsory jurisdiction, exercises continuous organization, and claims a monopoly of force over a territory and its population, including all action taking place in the area of jurisdiction."[64] Companies are involved in every aspect of the war effort, lobbying political parties to enter the conflict, the manufacture of weapons, constructing buildings, clearing war zones, providing utilities for civilians and manufacturers, washing laundry, managing sewage, training Iraqi forces, making vehicles, creating national banks, serving fast food, advising military strategists, rehabilitating soldiers, interrogating suspects, providing security services which engage in combat and even co-ordinating private contractors. When companies profit from the beginning to end of a conflict, from when the bombs start dropping until the targets are rebuilt, we need to ask who is really fighting the war, on whose behalf and who controls the state.

[60] MacAskill, E. (2010). *Barack Obama Ends the War in Iraq.* Available: http://www.guardian.co.uk/world/2010/sep/01/obama-formally-ends-iraq-war. Last accessed 17th Oct 2011.
[61] Congressional Research Service. (2011). *Department of Defense Contractors in Afghanistan and Iraq: Background and Analysis.* Available: www.fas.org/sgp/crs/natsec/R40764.pdf. Last accessed 13th Oct 2011.
[62] Risen, J. (2008). *Use of Iraq Contractors Costs Billions, Report Says.* Available: http://www.nytimes.com/2008/08/12/washington/12contractors.html. Last accessed 29th Dec 2011.
[63] Klein, N (2008). *The Shock Doctrine.* 2nd ed. London: Penguin Group. Pg. 316
[64] Kreijen, G (2004). *State Failure, Sovereignty and Effectiveness.* Oegstgeest: Brill Academic Publishers. Pg. 44

Chapter 1

"I think the real reasons behind the Iraq War lie in an almost… philosophical and geo-political vision of the neo-conservatives who dominate our foreign policy establishment today… That is the belief that the United States does dominate the world, as the world's sole superpower, that it must assert its power globally, everywhere, and that anyone who resists this or defies American power is absolutely unacceptable and becomes automatically, very much the enemy."[65]
> - Graham Fuller, former CIA Chief of Station in Kabul, Afghanistan

"I can't tell you if the use of force in Iraq today will last five days, five weeks or five months, but it won't last any longer than that."[66]
> - Donald Henry Rumsfeld, 2002

On the afternoon of September 10th 2001, Secretary of Defence Donald Rumsfeld delivered a speech at the Pentagon, less than twenty hours before American Airlines Flight 11 crashed into the North Tower of the World Trade Centre. He spoke of the bureaucracy of the Pentagon as an adversary posing a serious threat to the security of the United States, describing it as one of the "world's last bastions of central planning."[67] He called for the modernisation of the systems that control the Department of Defence, which according to some evidence, had been unable to track $2.3 trillion in transactions and were wasting between $3 billion and $4 billion annually.[68] He not only spoke of downsizing the department but of privatising whole areas of the military: "At bases around the world, why do we pick up our own garbage and mop our own floors, rather than contracting services out, as many businesses do?"[69] The aim, he illustrated, was to outsource work to the private sector who would then do the work more efficiently, reduce costs and allow troops to focus on their task of defending American interests. It appeared the military was to be treated more like an efficient corporation than a force administering government department. Rumsfeld's demands to outsource anything not inherently military were quickly followed up by General Tommy Franks and soon took effect during the War on Terror, beginning less than a month after his speech with the invasion of Afghanistan.

1.1 History of Private Military Contracting

Defence contractors, as business organisations providing products and services to the military department of the government, are not something new to the 21st Century. The United States has a history of war contracting, including the American Revolutionary War in the 18th Century where civil merchants provided supplies for troops. It stands to reason that where government

---

[65] Fuller, G. *Uncovered: The War on Iraq*. 2004. [DVD] Robert Greenwald, USA: Cinema Libre Studio.
[66] Cable News Network. (2002). *Rumsfeld: No World War III in Iraq*. Available: http://articles.cnn.com/2002-11-15/us/rumsfeld.iraq_1_iraq-air-patrols-surface-to-air-missiles?_s=PM:US. Last accessed 5th Jan 2012.
[67] U.S. Department of Defense. (2001). *Bureaucracy to Battlefield*. Available: http://www.defense.gov/speeches/speech.aspx?speechid=430. Last accessed 11th Oct 2011.
[68] Chatterjee, P (2009). *Halliburton's Army*. New York: Nation Books. Pg. xi-xii
[69] *Ibid*. Pg. xii

does not own the means of production, and simply purchases the wealth it requires for activity such as war, it must call upon private business to provide those resources. The scale of this contracting has colossal financial potential considering the logistics of modern warfare: "for every shooter out there, every man with a gun, there are hundreds behind supporting; providing the ammunition, the boots, the gas for the tanks, the oil."[70] In the case of the Iraq War private corporations went beyond merely providing services, and came to dominate the United States government's decision making. Companies, who went on to benefit greatly from the war, not only influenced the decision of the nation to enter the war but also the processes of selection for contracts from the military, and how those contracts were formalised. They managed this through both financial contributions to the Republican Party and by operating in government as well as the private sphere.

The Constitution of the United States defends the right of individuals to seek influence over their government. Stipulated in the First Amendment: "the congress shall make no laws respecting... the right of the people... to petition the government."[71] United States Congressman Ron Paul, who voted against the 2002 Iraq War Resolution,[72] argues that a lack of authority from the Congress is allowing power to be usurped by the President. "Since World War II, all our wars have been fought without a congressional declaration of war. It's the President who decides and the Congress that submits by appropriating the funds demanded. This Presidential authority was never intended by the Constitution."[73] He argues that the solution is for the Congress to strictly adhere to only that explicitly authorised in the Constitution, "there would be very little up for auction by the politicians, thus there would be little incentive to spend big lobbying bucks to gain special benefits."[74]Although the Constitution acts as a framework for the organisation of government, separating powers to focus duties and to keep check upon one another, it has been largely ignored. More and more legislation has empowered an elite to discount its stipulations with little protest. A fear of terrorism, exacerbated by the events of September 11th, has aided support for what could otherwise be seen as regressive policy-making.

---

[70] *Why We Fight*, 2005. [DVD] Eugene Jarecki, USA: Arte Films.
[71] Second Continental Congress (2008). *The Constitution of the United States of America with the Bill of Rights and all of the Amendments*. Virginia: Wilder Publications. Pg. 24
[72] Project Vote Smart. (2011). *Legislation: Representative Ronald 'Ron' Ernest Paul*. Available: http://www.votesmart.org/candidate/key-votes/296/. Last accessed 3rd Nov 2011.
[73] Paul, R (2011). *Liberty Defined*. New York: Grand Central Publishing. Pg. 111
[74] *Ibid*. Pg. 179

1.2 Laws Governing Private Military Companies

Following the Vietnam War, the War Powers Act of 1973 was legislated to "insure that the collective judgment of both the Congress and the President will apply to the introduction of United States Armed Forces into hostilities."[75] The document, which acted more as a bill than a resolution, allowed, among other abilities, the President as Commander-in-Chief to launch war without Congressional authority if they deemed it necessary following "a national emergency created by attack upon the United States".[76] It was this law, adopted seven days after the September 11th attacks, which allowed President George W. Bush to use all force necessary against the nations, organisations and individuals thought to have been involved in those attacks. Following an intelligence dossier published by the British government in 2002, which was later proven false,[77] the 'Authorization for the Use of Military Force Against Iraq Resolution' was enacted. This allowed the President to use the armed forces in any way deemed necessary to defend national security. George W. Bush's doctrine commanded intervention against foreign regimes that threatened the United States, implementation of global democratic policy, and the privatisation of all state-run businesses. Legislation such as the Iraq War Resolution, USA Patriot Act and National Security and Homeland Security Presidential Directive granted the President substantial unconstitutional authority. This unrestricted power combined with a neo-conservative agenda made George W. Bush and his administration the prime candidates to benefit special interest groups. As early as January 2001 Vice President Dick Cheney was holding meetings with the newly formed National Energy Policy Development Group, a panel composed largely of figures from leading oil companies including Conoco Inc. and BP plc.[78] Following the filing of a Freedom of Information Act upon the group by non-partisan foundation Judicial Watch, documents revealed "maps of Iraqi oilfields, with a long list of corporate 'suitors' for each oilfield."[79] This was eight months before the September 11th attacks created the pretext for war, and whilst Iraq's oil was under embargo by the United Nations. Military historian Tariq Ali describes the sale of the Iraq War to 'foreign exploiters' as "imperialism in the epoch of neo-liberal economics. Everything will be privatised, including civil society."[80] The Bush administration would institute many policies regarding Iraq which

---

[75] The Senate and the House of Representatives of the United States of America. (1973). *The War Powers Act of 1973.* Available: ocw.mit.edu/courses/political-science/17-471-american-national-security-policy-fall-2002/calendar/The_War_Powers_Act_of_1973.pdf - 2011-07-24. Last accessed 3rd Nov 2011. Pg. 1
[76] *Ibid.*
[77] Taylor, R. (2005). *We Got it Wrong on Iraq WMD, Intelligence Chiefs Finally Admit.* Available: http://www.guardian.co.uk/politics/2005/apr/08/uk.iraq. Last accessed 4th Nov 2011.
[78] Dubose, L; Bernstein, J (2006). *Vice.* New York: Random House Publishing Group. Pg. 7
[79] *Ibid.* Pg. 15
[80] Ali, T (2003). *Bush in Babylon.* London: Verso. Pg. 3

indeed proved to be exceedingly profitable. In the months leading up to invasion in the Spring of 2003, lobbyists, public relations counsellors and confidential advisors to senior public officials "marched together in the vanguard of those who advocated war."[81]

Back in 1985, under the administration of Ronald Reagan, an order was signed describing a new military doctrine called the Logistic Civilian Augmentation Program (LOGCAP). The program "set out the concepts, responsibilities, policies, and procedures for using civilian contractors to replace soldiers and recruiting local labour during war time,"[82] allowing civilians to profit from performing selected services to support the United States military. It was first used three years later, and is now the umbrella that private contractors such as DynCorp, Halliburton Company, KBR, Lockheed Martin and Blackwater Worldwide[83] are under, when called upon by governments to provide goods and services for military departments around the world. Briody argues that LOGCAP was corrupt from its roots. The entire design of the program derived from links with construction and engineering company Brown & Root, whose owners, George and Herman Brown, were personal friends of President Lyndon Baines Johnson. They provided him with illegal donations, he in turn deliberately administered policy in the company's favour.[84]

1.3 Halliburton Company and BearingPoint Inc.

Gideon Burrows argues that the arms trade is an exceedingly lucrative industry. It suffers from over-capacity in production resulting in fierce competition. Combined with the secrecy that surrounds matters of 'national interest' it becomes a 'breeding ground' for corruption.[85] This kind of secrecy, Lou Dubose and Jake Bernstein argue, in relation to the Bush Administration, is "operational policy for a government colluding with powerful corporate sponsors."[86] William Hartung, argues that a 'symbiotic relationship' has developed between the Pentagon and its top contractors. "The practice of doling out contracts according to the financial needs of the arms makers rather than the merits of a particular weapon design is a long-standing practice in the military-industrial complex."[87]

[81] Moore, M (2004). *The Official Fahrenheit 9/11 Reader*. New York: Simon & Schuster Inc. Pg. 304
[82] Chatterjee, P (2009). *Halliburton's Army*. New York: Nation Books. Pg. 52
[83] The company has since changed its name, first to Xe Services in 2009 and now to Academi as of 2011.
[84] Briody, D (2004). *The Halliburton Agenda*. New Jersey: John Wiley & Sons Inc. Pg. 120
[85] Gilby, N (2009). *The No-Nonsense Guide to the Arms Trade*. 2nd ed. Oxford: New Internationalist Publications Ltd. Pg. 99-100
[86] Dubose, L; Bernstein, J (2006). *Vice*. New York: Random House Publishing Group. Pg. 21
[87] Hartung, W (2011). *Prophets of War*. New York: Nation Books. Pg. 72

Naomi Wolf claims "the years following 9/11 have proved a bonanza for America's security contractors, with the Bush administration outsourcing areas of work that traditionally fell to the US military."[88] According to the non-profit organisation Center for Public Integrity, in the year 2003 alone oilfield services company Halliburton Company won over $4 billion to service the United States military in Afghanistan and Iraq.[89] The largest in-country corporation would go on to become the largest contract in Iraq,[90] an achievement made by a corporation with a long history of close government connections. It became legally incorporated in 1924 as an oil well company whose unique selling point was the prevention of dangers associated with high-pressure oil and gas extraction. It is now the second largest oilfield services corporation in the world[91] having acquired the construction, engineering and chemical engineering companies Brown & Root in 1962,[92] C. F. Braun Inc. in 1989,[93] M. W. Kellogg in 2001[94] and BE&K Inc. in 2008.[95] The companies it has absorbed have had similar backgrounds, starting out as businesses with expertises that serviced one department, but then expanded out to appeal to the military.

As noted above in their relationship with LOGCAP, Brown & Root, a construction company founded in 1919, have their roots in the lobbying of then-President Lyndon Baines Johnson. After the economic disaster of the Great Depression Johnson found himself being approached by "businessmen who wanted him to help them get New Deal dollars for their projects."[96] The company grew big on the back of this connection to Johnson. Through campaign contributions they received the government contracts they needed to remain profitable. The fruits of their labour paid off. The company won contracts with the United States military to provide services during the Vietnam War, Kosovo War, the War in Afghanistan, Operation Iraqi Freedom and has netted an estimated $9.7 million constructing Camp Delta, the U.S. Naval Base in Guantánamo Bay.[97] Since the War on Terror began, the ten-year LOGCAP III sole source cost-

[88] Wolf, N. (2007). Fascist America, in 10 Easy Steps. Available: http://www.guardian.co.uk/world/2007/apr/24/usa.comment. Last accessed 12th July 2011.
[89] Center for Public Integrity. (2011). *Outsourcing the Pentagon: Halliburton Co.* Available: http://projects.publicintegrity.org/pns/db.aspx?act=cinfo&coid=964409007. Last accessed 6th Nov 2011.
[90] Miller, T. (2007). *Private Contractors Outnumber US Troops in Iraq.* Available: http://www.commondreams.org/archive/2007/07/04/2284. Last accessed 4th Nov 2011.
[91] Press Release Distribution. (2009). *World's Top 10 Largest Oilfield Services Companies.* Available: http://www.prlog.org/10347986-worlds-top-10-largest-oilfield-services-companies.html. Last accessed 2nd June 2011.
[92] Briody, D (2004). *The Halliburton Agenda.* New Jersey: John Wiley & Sons Inc. Pg. 71
[93] The New York Times. (1989). *Halliburton Deal.* Available: http://www.nytimes.com/1989/06/17/business/company-news-halliburton-deal.html. Last accessed 2nd June 2011.
[94] Chatterjee, P (2009). *Halliburton's Army.* New York: Nation Books. Pg. 21
[95] Cooper, L. (2008). *Houston Company to Buy Birmingham's BE&K*. Available: http://www.bizjournals.com/birmingham/stories/2008/05/05/daily21.html. Last accessed 2nd June 2011.
[96] Chatterjee, P (2009). *Halliburton's Army.* New York: Nation Books. Pg. 15

plus contract has cleared Halliburton's subsidiary company KBR more than $25 billion,[98] causing the company's stock price to quadruple between March 2003 and January 2006.[99] The reliance that the United States military places upon this company is enormous. From the invasion onwards the corporation has performed tasks including building refineries, chemical plants and liquefied-natural-gas terminals as well as supporting the military through provision of meals, housing, fuel transport and mail delivery.[100]

Until its removal in 2011, situated forty-two miles north of Baghdad was the largest military base in all of Iraq, Joint Base Balad, formerly Logistical Support Area Anaconda, with thirty thousand workers within its fences.[101] The facility was built and is operated entirely by Halliburton Company/KBR, performing every task from housing soldiers and serving regular meals to manning watchtowers and graveling paths. In 2010 KBR was the largest U.S. Military contractor in Iraq with twenty four thousand employees,[102] as Sergeant Geoff Millard of the Army National Guard put it: "If you don't know KBR, you have never been to Iraq."[103]

In the early 1990s, Secretary of Defence under George H. W. Bush, Richard 'Dick' Cheney[104] was placed under pressure by the U.S. Congress to downsize the military and its bloated Cold War budgets.[105] He gave "Halliburton's subsidiary Brown & Root $3.9 million to compile a report showing how it could provide services to the U.S. military in assorted parts of the world."[106] Two years after leaving office at the Pentagon he became Chairman and Chief Executive Officer at that very company. "By paying Halliburton to run through the mock exercises back in 1992, he'd made it the most qualified for nearly all up coming Pentagon contracts."[107] Between 1995 and 2000 Cheney used his political clout in order to lobby government for it to intervene through policy, encouraging the lifting of sanctions on countries the company wanted to invest in.[108] Over a ninety year period Halliburton Company went from having a payroll of just fifty-

[97] Horrock, N; Iqbal, A. (2004). *Waiting for Gitmo.* Available: http://motherjones.com/politics/2004/01/waiting-gitmo. Last accessed 2nd June 2011.
[98] Chatterjee, P (2009). *Halliburton's Army.* New York: Nation Books. Pg. x
[99] Juhasz, A (2006). *The Bush Agenda.* New York: HarperCollins Publishers Inc. Pg. 6
[100] Kennett, J. (2006). *Halliburton's KBR Jumps 22% in First Day of Trading.* Available: http://www.bloomberg.com/apps/news?pid=newsarchive&sid=aiiAdkFc6I9U&refer=home. Last accessed 2nd June 2011.
[101] Chatterjee, P (2009). *Halliburton's Army.* New York: Nation Books. Pg. 140
[102] Chatterjee, P (2004). *Iraq, Inc.* Toronto: Seven Stories Press. Pg. 12
[103] *Iraq for Sale: The War Profiteers.* (2006) [DVD] United States: Brave New Films.
[104] Richard Bruce Cheney will be referred to in this study by his commonly used name Dick Cheney
[105] Briody, D (2004). *The Halliburton Agenda.* New Jersey: John Wiley & Sons Inc. Pg. 184
[106] Rossi, M (2009). *What Every American Should Know about Who's Really Running the World.* New York: Nation Books. Pg. 261
[107] *Ibid.*
[108] Chatterjee, P (2009). *Halliburton's Army.* New York: Nation Books. Pg. 42

six people to employing over fifty thousand people in approximately eighty countries around the world.[109] The company and its former subsidiary KBR are by far the largest recipients of contracts for both the Iraq and Afghanistan wars.[110] In the five years before Dick Cheney took up his position at the head of the company Halliburton made $100 million in government credit guarantees. It made $1.5 billion in the five years he was there.[111] The route that Halliburton took to achieve its current status aids an understanding of the 2003 Iraq War as an inevitable consequence of the relationship between the state, the military, private contractors and the immense revenue war can create.

Despite being too young to be granted early retirement under his contract, Dick Cheney received the privilege in 2000 and was able to join George W. Bush in the presidential election race. Whilst fulfilling his role as Vice President, Cheney continued to receive payments from Halliburton, a total of $952,444 between 2001 and 2005[112] in what was termed 'deferred compensation'.[113] A report by the Congressional Research Service says these deferred payments, along with his possession of stock options, could be seen as 'ties' or 'linkages to former employers' that may "represent a continuing financial interest in those employers which makes them potential conflicts of interest."[114] Cheney effectively operated within the revolving door of politics, moving from his role in the regulation of industry into a company directly affected by that regulation. He waited the necessary amount of time to make his actions legal with regard to conflict of interest laws. However the impact he had on the relationship between the private sector and government is a major factor in understanding the Iraq War. The Bush administration continually allowed for the prosperity of special interests to outweigh the needs of the citizenry. This drive for profit, and potential for exploitation, meant extensive lobbying of government occurred prior to the war. Former Senior Vice President of the World Bank, Joseph Stiglitz, says that "in America, corruption takes on a more nuanced form than it does elsewhere. Payoffs typically do not take the form of direct bribes, but of campaign contributions to both parties."[115] Companies that gave considerable campaign contributions were granted contracts for military services even if they were not selected by merit or because they offered the lowest bid. They

[109] Halliburton. (2012). *Community.* Available: http://www.halliburton.com/AboutUs/default.aspx?navid=982&pageid=2349. Last accessed 2nd Jan 2012.
[110] Verlöy, A; Politi, D. (2004). *Halliburton Contracts Balloon.* Available: http://www.iwatchnews.org/national-security/windfalls-war. Last accessed 3rd Sep 2010.
[111] Chatterjee, P (2009). *Halliburton's Army.* New York: Nation Books. Pg. 49
[112] Chatterjee, P (2009). *Halliburton's Army.* New York: Nation Books. Pg. 49
[113] BBC News. (2001). *Cheney's Millions Dwarf Bush Income.* Available: http://news.bbc.co.uk/1/hi/world/americas/1277968.stm. Last accessed 3rd Sep 2011.
[114] Halliburton Watch. (2011). *Cheney Violates Ethics Law.* Available: http://www.halliburtonwatch.org/about_hal/ethics.html. Last accessed 29th Dec 2011.
[115] Stiglitz, J; Bilmes, L (2008). *The Three Trillion Dollar War.* London: Penguin Group. Pg. 15

continued to provide contributions during the war and continue to have their contracts renewed. According to the Center for Responsive Politics the management and technology consulting firm BearingPoint Inc. spent an estimated $1 million lobbying government in 2003.[116] That same year the company were awarded a $9 million contract to plan and introduce a new currency to Iraq with the declared intention being that of organising small loans to Iraqi entrepreneurs to stimulate the market economy.[117] Public integrity watchdogs criticised the way the company was awarded the contract as "BearingPoint advisers to USAID [United States Agency for International Development] had a hand in drafting the requirements set out in the tender,"[118] spending months helping USAID write the specifications of the project "while its competitors had only a week to read the specifications and submit their own bids after final revisions were made."[119] They effectively excluded competition from the bid and secured themselves enormous profits in the process. This failure to find an appropriate contractor resulted in an audit performed by the Office of Inspector General USAID showing that six years after the contract was issued the company had still failed to implement the necessary financial systems, with the total amount spent on the project estimated at $37.4 million.[120]

1.4 Consequences of LOGCAP

LOGCAP initially may have intended to use the private sector to perform tasks more efficiently and to lower costs for the benefit of the state and public interest. In fact it made contracts with the military exceedingly profitable. Rumsfeld's plans to outsource functions the military traditionally performed created an environment where a company could monopolise services to the government for enormous profit. This pursuit of profit opened the government to intense lobbying. A government granted exceptional powers through post-Vietnam and post-9/11 legislation, that in no way adhered to the Constitution, allowed commercial interests to benefit from regulatory capture. The government agency regulating the industry became "dominated by the interests of the industries that they are suppose to oversee."[121] Their interests were advanced by the decisions government made, resulting in the negative externalities warfare causes.

[116] Center for Responsive Politics. (2003). *Influence and Lobbying: BearingPoint Inc.* Available: http://www.opensecrets.org/lobby/clientsum.php?id=D000024292&year=2003. Last accessed 3rd Sep 2011.
[117] McDougall, P. (2003). *BearingPoint Gears Up For Iraq Rebuilding.* Available: http://www.informationweek.com/news/12808110. Last accessed 12th Jul 2011.
[118] Foley, S. (2007). *Shock and Oil: Iraq's Billions & the White House Connection.* Available: http://www.independent.co.uk/news/world/americas/shock-and-oil-iraqs-billions-amp-the-white-house-connection-431977.html. Last accessed 12th July 2011.
[119] *Ibid.*
[120] Office of Inspector General. (2010). *Audit of USAID/Iraq's Implementation of the Iraq Financial Management Information System.* Available: pdf.usaid.gov/pdf_docs/PDACS038.pdf. Last accessed 1st Jan 2012.
[121] Devine, T; Maassarani, T (2011). *The Corporate Whistleblower's Survival Guide.* California: Berrett-Koehler Publishers Inc. Pg. 91

Essentially the Bush Administration was operating as a 'corporatocracy' with regard to Iraq. Corporations to a significant extent wield power over government, retaining "the superficial appearance of being a democratic republic... but below the surface, it is a system of government without full and true representation of the people."[122]

Before the war the legislation was in place for Iraq to become a huge investment for corporations and long before the first missiles struck Baghdad contracts were being issued to companies. Chapter Two will examine what happened next, what the contracts specified, how they were abused and the consequences of those abuses.

Chapter 2

---

[122] Bartz, S (2011). *The Tylenol Mafia*. New York: New Light Publishing. Pg. 338

"The great beneficiaries of the Age of Terrorism aren't the terrorists themselves, but the governments who use the tools of fear to intimidate and control their people."[123]
- Melissa Rossi, American Author and Journalist

"Experience has shown that only rulers and republics that possess their own armies are very successful, whereas mercenary armies never achieve anything, and cause only harm."[124]
- Niccolò dei Machiavelli, Italian Philosopher, 1532 AD

On March 20th 2003, at 5.33 a.m. local time, the United States Central Intelligence Agency's Special Activities Division called in air strikes on the Iraqi capital of Baghdad to begin the invasion. At least ten thousand Iraqis were killed in these initial attacks.[125] Later that day General Tommy Franks, commander of the United States Armed Forces, would report that after the first full day of warfare there were 241,516 U.S. military personnel in the region[126] and that "Special Forces were in partial control of the vast western desert – 25 percent of Iraq's territory."[127] Although congressional approval for the use of military force against Iraq did not come until October 2002, ships had begun delivering military equipment into Kuwait in August. Private military companies soon after began constructing buildings for the army to operate from.[128] When the invasion occurred aircraft were not being deployed from, or refuelling in, bases within the United States but at military bases located far closer to Iraq, such as the island of Diego Garcia in the centre of the Indian Ocean.[129] Exactly thirty years before aircraft departed the island bound for Baghdad, Halliburton Company had been commissioned to build the base there,[130] expanding a pre-existing airfield into an enormous facility which included stations for submarines and naval ships, hangars to house fleets of jets, runways and maintenance buildings. David Vine argues that the base at Diego Garcia, and its use in the conflicts in Iraq and Afghanistan, show how "these wars were… the fulfilment of a strategic vision for controlling a large swathe of Asia and, with it, the global economy… The wars have significantly advanced the pursuit of U.S. control over Central Asian and Persian Gulf oil and natural gas supplies through the presence of hundreds of thousands of U.S. troops and private military contractors."[131] It was necessary that bases such as these had already been established for warfare on strategic targets within the Middle East and Central Asia. Without their construction by private

---

[123] Rossi, M (2009). *What Every American Should Know about Who's Really Running the World*. New York: Nation Books. Pg. 353
[124] Machiavelli, N (1993). *Machiavelli: The Prince*. 5th ed. Cambridge: Cambridge University Press. Pg. 44
[125] Polk, W (2005). *Understanding Iraq*. London: I.B.Tauris & Co Ltd. Pg. 3
[126] Along with 41,000 troops from the United Kingdom and 2,200 from other nations that form the Coalition of the Willing.
[127] Woodward, B (2004). *Plan of Attack*. New York: Simon & Schuster Inc. Pg. 401
[128] Chatterjee, P (2009). *Halliburton's Army*. New York: Nation Books. Pg. 79
[129] Pilger, J (2002). *The New Rulers of the World*. London: Verso. Pg. 132
[130] Chatterjee, P (2009). *Halliburton's Army*. New York: Nation Books. Pg. 53
[131] Vine, D (2011). *Island of Shame*. 4th ed. New Jersey: Princeton University Press. Pg. 188

businesses wars thousands of miles from the United States would either be exponentially more costly than currently or entirely unfeasible.

2.1 The Role of Private Contractors

The movement of military cargo before congressional authorisation of war, and the issuing of contracts in advance of invasion, were highly unusual events. During the planning for the war Secretary of Defence Donald Rumsfeld had demanded from both General Franks and the commander of the United States Air Force, General Victor Renuart, that the invasion force should not number more than one hundred and fifty thousand.[132] Franks had estimated that there would need to be at least two hundred and forty-five thousand ground troops alone to secure not just the toppling of Saddam Hussein's regime, but a stable post-invasion occupation.[133] It was this pressure to reduce numbers that saw contracts being drawn up so early, with 3,512 security contracts issued in 2003 alone.[134] Private corporations stepped in to perform tasks the military was not willing to commit men to, or increase numbers where they lacked strength. Effectively it was "Halliburton/KBR that would expand to take up the slack."[135] A key example of this was the contracting of Halliburton, prior to the war, to extinguish oil well fires the invading US-led Coalition predicted the retreating Iraqi forces would light. When those fires did not occur, Halliburton's contract was extended to perform dozen of other military functions that did need doing, such as national provision of oil and vehicle maintenance.[136]

Oilfield services weren't the only industry that had their roles extended. Across the board the roles of private corporations expanded beyond their initial provisions. Private military company Blackwater Worldwide initially received a $27 million no-bid contract in 2003 to provide security for the Administrator of the Coalition Provisional Authority, Lewis Paul Bremer.[137] It had increased to $100 million by 2004 and went even further in 2007, becoming a $1.2 billion contract to provide 'diplomatic security' in all of Iraq.[138] The term the Bush administration used to describe nations that supported, verbally or militarily, the invasion of Iraq in 2003 was the 'Coalition of the Willing'. Robert Young Pelton claims that as the escalating cost of the conflict caused members of 'Multi-National Force – Iraq' to withdraw, that military command should

[132] Chatterjee, P (2009). *Halliburton's Army*. New York: Nation Books. Pg. 79
[133] Woodward, B (2004). *Plan of Attack*. New York: Simon & Schuster Inc. Pg. 82
[134] Klein, N (2008). *The Shock Doctrine*. 2nd ed. London: Penguin Group. Pg. 12
[135] Chatterjee, P (2009). *Halliburton's Army*. New York: Nation Books. Pg. 79
[136] Klein, N (2008). *The Shock Doctrine*. 2nd ed. London: Penguin Group. Pg. 379
[137] Scahill, J (2007). *Blackwater*. 2nd ed. London: Perseus Books Group. Pg. 13
[138] Stiglitz, J; Bilmes, L (2008). *The Three Trillion Dollar War*. London: Penguin Group. Pg. 12

more appropriately have been called the 'Coalition of the Billing'. "We've never done this in any war up until this point, we've never physically paid for companies to replace countries."[139]

The use of private military contractors supposedly has enormous financial and legal benefits for the military. CACI International Inc., a major recipient of Iraq War contracts, says private contracting saves the taxpayer money by employing business 'as needed' rather than "maintaining military salaries and benefits year round, year after year... When contractor services are no longer required they can be cut back quickly."[140] Employees do not cost the government in pensions or full-time workers needs, the government is not held accountable if they are captured and because the employees are accountable only to their company, the military do not need to declare their operations or even their existence. This means that private companies can be used in secretive operations, outside of media scrutiny and leave the image of the military untarnished. Kevin O'Brien argues "by privatizing security and the use of violence, removing it from the domain of the state and giving it to private interest, the state in these instances is both being strengthened and disassembled."[141] Where they can operate covertly and at a reduced cost, private companies are undermining state sovereignty over its military and the actions taken on behalf of the nation. Naomi Klein argues that the Bush administration used the September 11th attacks not simply as justification for a global War on Terror but that the war would be "an almost completely for-profit venture, a booming new industry that has breathed new life into the faltering U.S. economy."[142]

2.2 Cost-Plus Contracts

Many of the contracts issued for work in Iraq were cost-plus. Essentially these stipulate that the contractor is paid for all of its allowed expenses to an agreed limit, plus additional payment which allows for a profit, rather than being paid a predetermined amount regardless of incurred expenses. Briody puts it that with regard to the conditions of a cost-plus contract "even a layman can tell that means good things from the contractor... Basically, it's a blank check [sic] from the government."[143] Peter Singer, claims "the rationale in choosing a cost-type contract for buying military logistical support is that it provides the flexibility necessary to support operations where mission requirements may change frequently."[144] This is exactly what occurred with the contract

[139] Pelton, R. *Shadow Company*, 2006. [DVD] Nick Bicanic, Jason Bourque, Canada: Purpose Films.
[140] CACI International Inc. (2011). *Truth and Error in the Media Portrayal of CACI in Iraq.* Available: http://www.caci.com/iraq/truth_error.shtml. Last accessed 15th July 2011.
[141] O'Brien, K, "Military-Advisory Groups and African Security: Privatised Peacekeeping," *International Peacekeeping*, Vol. 5, No. 3 (Autumn 1998). Pg. 78
[142] Klein, N (2008). *The Shock Doctrine.* 2nd ed. London: Penguin Group. Pg. 12
[143] Briody, D (2004). *The Halliburton Agenda.* New Jersey: John Wiley & Sons Inc. Pg. 185
[144] Singer, P (2008). *Corporate Warriors.* 2nd ed. New York: Cornell University Press. Pg. 141

expansions of Halliburton Company, Bechtel Group and Blackwater Worldwide. The final cost of cost-plus contracts became unpredictable. This resulted in private companies overcharging for goods and services provided to Coalition forces. In the case of Iraq the costs were being accounted for by the United States Department of Defence, an enormous bureaucracy for which the task proved difficult, especially where the bodies needed to perform the task lacked manpower or ceased to exist altogether. In 2008 there were only seventeen personnel in its contract compliance department overseeing $4 billion worth of contracts.[145]

2.3 The True Cost of Contracts

In the arena of warfare, where a situation can change drastically in a very short period of time, the company being contracted must require minimal assistance from its client government and have a global presence to deal with any eventuality. "The firm must have the financial capacity to operate on this large scale for up to 60 days without reimbursement, given the time required to set up complex financial systems to pay for the services."[146] The difficulty with this necessity is that only a handful of enormous conglomerates could meet it in 2003. This included Halliburton Company, who had benefitted from their extensive training prior to the implementation of LOGCAP. With a small selection of corporations in control of Iraq's reconstruction, it fell to their discretion which companies would be subcontracted to perform tasks. There was high unemployment in Iraq following the 2003 invasion, resulting in poor living standards and civil unrest. A cost-effective solution to this problem would have been to hire the domestic population to aid the reconstruction of their own nation. This did not occur. In May 2004 the Pentagon's Program Management Office in Baghdad reported that of a workforce of seven million, less than one percent were employed in rebuilding projects.[147] Companies could employ whomever they deemed fit for the job, without considering the cost because their profits were secured through the nature of their contracts. The lack of local labour suggests foreign companies and the occupying powers did not employ Iraqis due to a lack of trust. When KBR were tasked with providing a laundry service for the military "instead of finding a laundry in Baghdad or hiring Iraqis to wash items by hand, KBR sent the garments to Kuwait."[148] Unemployment reached 67% in 2004, that same year the Ministry of Industry admitted that of the seventeen state-owned cement factories in Iraq none had received contracts from the United States to aid reconstruction of the country even though they had proven their ability to produce

[145] Stiglitz, J; Bilmes, L (2008). *The Three Trillion Dollar War*. London: Penguin Group. Pg. 14
[146] Singer, P (2008). *Corporate Warriors*. 2nd ed. New York: Cornell University Press. Pg. 141
[147] Chatterjee, P (2004). *Iraq, Inc*. Toronto: Seven Stories Press. Pg. 12
[148] Chandrasekaran, R (2008). *Imperial Life in the Emerald City*. London: Bloomsbury Publishing Plc. Pg. 54

blast walls ten times cheaper than importers.[149] Cost-plus contracts made it possible for companies to pay additional costs to use foreign labour and goods, just for security reasons. Klein writes: "Imported products and foreign workers flooding across the borders have become a source of tremendous resentment in Iraq and yet another open tap fueling the insurgency."[150] Cost-plus contracts made it possible for companies to pay additional costs to use foreign labour and goods for 'security reasons'.

2.4 Overcharging and Incomplete Projects

To accelerate efforts in Iraq, President Bush informed General Tommy Franks that the reconstruction costs could be whatever they were as long as the work was being done. "Franks told his commanders to inform him as to what they needed... So if they needed to do work on a combat vehicle ramp in Kuwait that would cost several million, just do it. Same with extending a runway in Oman. Or pouring concrete in Jordan. Do it."[151] *The Wall Street Journal* reported that the military had been overcharged up to $16 million by Halliburton in 2003, when the company accounted for 28,000 meals it had not actually served.[152] Whistleblower and former logistics specialist for Halliburton's subsidiary company KBR, Marie deYoung, went to the House Committee of Government Reform in 2004 claiming the company were exploiting their position as a service provider to the military and had delivered $1.4 billion in 'questioned' or 'unsupported' charges.[153] Chairman and CEO David Lesar defended the company against claims it was deliberately inflating costs to increase profits, by arguing that the overcharging was not intended but was caused by the chaotic nature of the business. "This is not, 'Can you do this for me in two months?' This is, 'Can you do this by the morning?'"[154] Deliberate or accidental, with so many aspects of the war effort having been privatised, overbilling occurred on a vast scale, the majority of which took a long time to uncover. It sometimes took independent organisations or investigative journalism to make the discoveries, and the amount of inflated costs that were not accounted for will never be known. Public Warehousing Corporation (PWC), now rebranded Agility Logistics, was investigated by the federal government over a contract it held to supply the military with meat. The findings concluded the company had overcharged the Pentagon as much as $374 million "by inserting a related company to inflate the amount billed."[155] The

[149] Klein, N (2004) 'Baghdad Year Zero'. *Harper's Magazine*. September, 2004. Pg. 49
[150] *Ibid.*
[151] Woodward, B (2004). *Plan of Attack*. New York: Simon & Schuster Inc. Pg. 123
[152] King, N 'Halliburton Hits Snafu on Billing in Kuwait,' *The Wall Street Journal*, 2 February 2003.
[153] Hickey, B. (2005). *Ms. deYoung Goes to Washington*. Available: http://archives.citypaper.net/articles/2005-07-28/cover.shtml. Last accessed 17th Aug 2011.
[154] Gold, R 'Halliburton Unit Runs into Big Obstacles in Iraq,' *The Wall Street Journal*, April 28, 2004.
[155] Simpson, C; Simpson, G 'How Iraq Conflict Reward a Kuwaiti Merchant Family,' *The Wall Street Journal*, December 17, 2007.

technique they had used, incentivised by the prospect of profiteering through the cost-plus contract model, used 'prompt payment discounts'. These discounts came in the form of a fee the contracted company attached to the goods it had to purchase from another company, before then selling those goods to the military. This additional cost was paid for by the military. In the case of PWC, and many others, both companies involved were in fact subsidiaries of the same parent company. The costs were being deliberately inflated, creating larger profits and unnecessary expense for the taxpayer. With enormous contracts over long periods of times, small additional fees could be placed on the sale of each item and yield enormous additional profits with little oversight.

In March 2004, engineering and construction firm Parsons Corporation, were awarded a $243 million project to construct one hundred and fifty health care centres across Iraq. Two years later over 75% of the allocated funds had been spent, only six centres had been fully constructed, with one hundred and thirty-five left partially complete. As a result the contract was cancelled and some of the projects given to other contractors to complete. Eventually one hundred and twenty-one of the constructions Parsons did continue to control were terminated after only being partially constructed due to funding problems.[156] In 2011, Saudi newspaper *Arab News* reported "the US government is currently spending $12 billion a month in Iraq, much of it with little accountability or oversight. Projects are plagued by cost overruns, poor record keeping, high turnover and criminally shoddy work."[157]

2.5 Sole Source Contracts and Monopolisation

Many of the contracts issued by the United States military for tasks in Iraq were 'sole source' or 'no-bid' in which competitive bidding for the contract does not occur because the implication is that there is only a certain company available with the capacity to meet the requirement. The Bush administration claimed they needed to act expeditiously with regard to Iraq, and that competitive bidding would slow the process down.[158] Former Deputy of Defence under President Ronald Reagan, Frank Carlucci, who went on to become Chairman of global asset management firm The Carlyle Group, pursued policies which yielded higher profits for the defence industry using "long-term and no-bid contracts, both moves intended to encourage private companies to enter the market."[159] In the matter of national interest and with compelling

---

[156] Mandel, J. (2006). *Report Details Problems with Contract for Iraq Health Centers.* Available: http://www.govexec.com/dailyfed/0506/050106m1.htm. Last accessed 12th Dec 2011.
[157] Ferguson, B. (2008). *Private contractors steal billions from Uncle Sam.* Available: http://archive.arabnews.com/?page=4&section=0&article=112255&d=30&m=7&y=2008. Last accessed 21st, July 2011.
[158] Stiglitz, J; Bilmes, L (2008). *The Three Trillion Dollar War*. London: Penguin Group. Pg. 13

urgency, the United States permits the awarding of sole source contracts by the government. Joseph Stiglitz claims that "Rumsfeld's refusal to allow competitive bidding for billions of dollars of reconstruction money – instead, relying on the usual cabal of Washington Beltway defense contractors – led to delays that resulted in a plummeting standard of living and squandering of our only real opportunity to win the hearts and minds of the Iraqi people."[160] When Halliburton/KBR were placing purchase orders for less than $2,500 they were only legally required to solicit one bid from one source. Henry Bunting, a former contract manager for the company, testified before the United States Senate Democratic Policy Committee that competitive bidding was deliberately avoided by breaking down requisitions into amounts below $2,500. These 'split orders' were then procured from 'preferred suppliers' even if the suppliers' ability to fulfil the order was non-competitive in pricing.[161] In court Bunting showed a towel the company has purchased for troops in a military facility in Baghdad, initially costing $1.60 Halliburton had insisted upon each item being stitched with an embroidered logo and had subsequently charged the government for the increased price of $7.50.[162] This process allowed individuals within the company to abuse the system by subcontracting to companies that had bribed them or offered the provision of 'kickbacks'.[163] This culture of bribery and corruption, in part due to the nature of the contracts, led to the mismanagement which left Iraq with sectarian violence, a lack of infrastructure and little hope of its reconstruction any time soon. As Klein writes, "if within six months of the invasion, Iraqis had found themselves drinking clean water from Bechtel pipes, their homes illuminated by GE [General Electric] lights, their infirm treated in sanitary Parsons-built hospitals, their streets patrolled by competent DynCorp-trained police, many citizens (though not all) would probably have overcome their anger at being excluded from the reconstruction process. But none of this happened, and well before Iraqi resistance forces began systematically targeting reconstruction sites it was clear that applying laissez-faire principles to such a huge government task had been a disaster."[164]

Chapter Three examines the role of private contractors in the rise of the Iraqi insurgency, the lives lost due to their mismanagement, and the consequences of privatising military functions.

Chapter 3

---

[159] Briody, D (2003). *The Iron Triangle*. New Jersey: John Wiley & Sons. Pg. 42

[160] Stiglitz, J; Bilmes, L (2008). *The Three Trillion Dollar War*. London: Penguin Group. Pg. 177

[161] Chatterjee, P (2009). *Halliburton's Army*. New York: Nation Books. Pg. 183

[162] Carlson, M. (2006). *Halliburton's Fleecing Ends - Or Does It?*. Available: http://www.bloomberg.com/apps/news?pid=newsarchive&refer=columnist_carlson&sid=aWq.XoaVqS4U. Last accessed 3rd Sep 2010.

[163] Chatterjee, P (2009). *Halliburton's Army*. New York: Nation Books. Pg. 200

[164] Klein, N (2008). *The Shock Doctrine*. 2nd ed. London: Penguin Group. Pg. 356

"The desire for exclusive markets is one of the most potent causes of war."[165]
- Betrand Russell, British Philosopher and Historian

"Why don't those damned oil companies fly their own flags on their personal property – maybe a flag with a gas pump on it."[166]
- Smedley Butler, Major General in the United States Marine Corps, 1937

Following President George W. Bush's announcement on March 19th 2003 that military operations had begun "to disarm Iraq, to free its people and to defend the world from grave danger,"[167] a state where the government had previously monopolised industry was opened up to foreign investment. The imposition in April 1991 of Security Council Resolution 687, following the Persian Gulf War, had banned Iraq from importing or exporting goods and had placed the country in enormous debt due, in part, to the reparations it had to pay Kuwait for its invasion in 1990.[168] Iraq was placed in a veritable 'catch-22', unable to make the financial compensations with the sanctions in place, and unable to lift the sanctions until it had compensated Kuwait. Although the sanctions were intended to destabilise the regime of Saddam Hussein it was the "general population rather than the core supporters [who] suffered."[169] Malnutrition and death occurred, due to a decreasing supply of food and a shortage of medical supplies.[170] Between 1991 and 1998 it is estimated the sanctions killed over 790,000 Iraqi children under the age of five.[171] Former Mujahideen soldier Osama bin Laden cited this as one of his reasons for opposing and fighting the United States.[172][173] The removal of these sanctions following the 2003 invasion allowed investors to receive no-bid, cost-plus contracts either to service the military, start new businesses or to operate one of the two hundred previously state-owned companies.

3.1 Lewis Paul Bremer's 'Free Market'

---

[165] Russell, B (1963). *Political Ideals*. London: George Allen & Unwin Publishers Ltd. Pg. 72
[166] Butler, S (2003). *War is a Racket*. 2nd ed. Los Angeles: Feral House. Pg. 1
[167] Suskind, R (2007). *The One Percent Doctrine*. 2nd ed. London: Pocket Books. Pg. 211
[168] Polk, W (2005). *Understanding Iraq*. London: I.B.Tauris & Co Ltd. Pg. 157
[169] *Ibid.* Pg. 158
[170] German, L (2001). *Anti-Capitalism*. 2nd ed. Sydney: Bath Press. Pg. 128
[171] Ali, M; Blacker, J; Jones, G. (2003). Annual Mortality Rates and Excess Deaths of Children under Five in Iraq, 1991-98. *Population Studies*. 57 (2), 223.
[172] The Guardian. (2002). *Full Text: Bin Laden's 'Letter to America'*. Available: http://www.guardian.co.uk/world/2002/nov/24/theobserver. Last accessed 18th Sep 2011.
[173] Ricks, T (2007). *Fiasco*. London: Penguin Group. Pg. 18

Paul Bremer, who was appointed the Administrator of the Coalition Provisional Authority (CPA) in 2003, immediately issued a series of decrees including Order 37, which lowered the corporate tax rate of the country from 40% to a flat 15%.[174] In September he issued Order 39 stipulating that property could be licensed for up to forty years, and be renewed beyond that.[175] "Overnight, Iraq went from being one of the most isolated countries in the world, sealed off from the most basic trade by strict UN sanctions, to becoming the widest-open market anywhere."[176] Paul Bremer told Rajiv Chandrasekaran, a journalist for *The Washington Post*, that economic reform was his top priority. He wanted to "corporatize and privatize state-owned enterprises... Saddam's government owned hundreds of factories. It subsidized the cost of gasoline, electricity, and fertilizer. Every family received monthly food rations. Bremer regarded all of that as unsustainable... [He] had come to Iraq to build not just a democracy but a free market."[177]

3.2 Consequences of the CPA Orders

The privatisation of state-owned businesses meant many individuals were dismissed as the companies downsized, creating rising unemployment as a labour force, entirely dependent on their wages to survive, rapidly lost their jobs. Amazia Baram, a former advisor to the Bush administration, claims: "there were people who were kicked out of their jobs even though they were just professionals, engineers, directors."[178] This was compounded when Bremer decreed CPA Order 1, 'de-Ba`athification', which attempted to remove the Ba'ath Party influence from the new Iraqi political system. It called for all public sector employees affiliated with the Ba'ath Party to be "removed from their positions and banned from future employment in the public sector."[179] The Iraq Study Group, a bipartisan panel appointed by the United States Congress, published a report in 2006 concluding that this policy insured "most of Iraq's technocratic class was pushed out of the government... Other skilled Iraqis have fled the country as violence has risen."[180] Many of the estimated 50,000 who fell victim to the policy were faced with permanent

[174] Coalition Provisional Authority. 2003. *Coalition Provisional Authority Order Number 37*. Pg. 3. [ONLINE] Available at: www.iraqcoalition.org/regulations/20030919_CPAORD_37_Tax_Strategy_for_2003.pdf. [Accessed 03 December 11].

[175] Coalition Provisional Authority. 2003. *Coalition Provisional Authority Order Number 39*. Pg. 5. [ONLINE] Available at: www.iraqcoalition.org/regulations/20031220_CPAORD_39_Foreign_Investment_.pdf. [Accessed 03 December 11].

[176] Klein, N (2008). *The Shock Doctrine*. 2nd ed. London: Penguin Group. Pg. 339

[177] Chandrasekaran, R (2008). *Imperial Life in the Emerald City*. London: Bloomsbury Publishing Plc. Pg. 68

[178] Baram, A. *No End in Sight*, 2007. [DVD] Charles Ferguson, USA: Representational Pictures.

[179] Coalition Provisional Authority. 2003. *Coalition Provisional Authority Order Number 1*. Pg. 1-2. [ONLINE] Available at: www.iraqcoalition.org/regulations/20030516_CPAORD_1_De-Ba_athification_of_Iraqi_Society_.pdf. [Accessed 03 December 11].

[180] Baker, J; Hamilton, L (2006). *The Iraq Study Group Report*. New York: Vintage Books. Pg. 21

unemployment. They had been essential to the Iraqi government, education system and economy; many of them had only joined the party simply to survive.[181]

These policies extended to the Iraqi military. As Director of the Office for Reconstruction and Humanitarian Assistance (ORHA), General Jay Garner, had initially proposed in 2003 that the Iraqi military units remaining after the invasion would be converted into labour corps, paid to carry out emergency repairs. When the Coalition Provisional Authority replaced ORHA after four months, the new administrator Paul Bremer reversed this policy. In May 2003 CPA Order 2 described entities of the prior Iraqi regime that would be 'dissolved', including the military, security and intelligence organisations.[182] The legislation "dismissed hundreds of thousands of soldiers, sending them home, ragged, hungry, and broke – but allowing them to keep their weapons… For Bremer's policy, the American army paid in blood."[183] Groups of distressed individuals resorted to crime to survive. The ensuing riots and looting resulted in death, displacement, theft of thousands of historical objects,[184] caused the destruction of systems that could provide basic amenities[185] and led to at least three days of looting without intervention.[186] Klein argues, "[Paul Bremer's] mission never was to win Iraqi hearts and minds. Rather, it was to get the country ready for the launch of Iraq Inc."[187]

The response was predictable. Prior to his rise as an Islamic political leader, Shi'a cleric Muqtada al-Sadr co-ordinated a donation-funded network of individuals who provided services to the local population including blood donation, traffic direction and generators for electricity.[188] He also armed and directed a paramilitary force known as the 'Mahdi Army' against Coalition forces, which comprised of as many as 60,000 fighters in 2006.[189] Through provision of services and the building of a political community he gave a practical alternative to the failing system implemented by the United States.

3.3 Immunity of Private Military and Security Contractors

[181] *No End in Sight*, 2007. [DVD] Charles Ferguson, USA: Representational Pictures.

[182] Coalition Provisional Authority. 2003. *Coalition Provisional Authority Order Number 2*. [ONLINE] Available at: www.iraqcoalition.org/regulations/20030823_CPAORD_2_Dissolution_of_Entities_with_Annex_A.pdf. [Accessed 03 December 11].

[183] Polk, W (2005). *Understanding Iraq*. London: I.B.Tauris & Co Ltd. Pg. 198 - 199

[184] BBC News. (2003). *'One in 10' Iraqi Treasures Looted*. Available: http://news.bbc.co.uk/1/hi/entertainment/arts/3054974.stm. Last accessed 6th Nov 2011.

[185] Baker, R; Ismael, S; and Ismael, T (2010). *Cultural Cleansing in Iraq*. New York: Pluto Press. Pg. 4

[186] Stone, P; Bajjaly J (2008). *The Destruction of Cultural Heritage in Iraq*. Suffolk: The Bodywell Press. Pg. 102

[187] Klein, N (2008). *The Shock Doctrine*. 2nd ed. London: Penguin Group. Pg. 344

[188] Klein, N (2004) 'Baghdad Year Zero'. *Harper's Magazine*. September, 2004. Pg. 49

[189] Baker, J; Hamilton, L (2006). *The Iraq Study Group Report*. New York: Vintage Books. Pg. 5

The escalating violence allowed for private military and security companies to sell their services to all those threatened groups on the ground that had invested in this new marketplace. Blackwater Worldwide, just one of more than one hundred and seventy 'mercenary' firms offering its services in Iraq. The company received just $204,000 in government contracts in 2000; eight years later their profits exceed $1 billion.[190] These private contractors had effectively been granted immunity from prosecution under CPA Order 17, which stipulated "contractors shall not be subject to Iraqi laws or regulations."[191] The implementation of this legislation, along with many other CPA orders, conflicted with international law, especially with regard to the ownership of state assets and the application of national law during wartime under the Third Geneva Convention and the Hague Conventions. As such there was reluctance from corporate interests to invest in Iraq. The CPA Orders decreed in May 2003, were finally legitimised by the dissolution of the Coalition Provisional Authority and the establishment of the National Assembly of Iraq in June 2005. The changes to the Constitution of Iraq included the incorporation of all CPA Orders. Klein argues that the return of sovereignty to the newly appointed Iraqi government was a transfer of power to a 'puppet regime' and was done to legalise the CPA decisions.[192] This lack of legal accountability was highlighted in September 2007 when employees of Blackwater USA shot and killed seventeen Iraqi civilians at a public square in Baghdad. It was difficult to bring criminal charges against the individuals involved due to the complexity of conflicting legislation. Despite Blackwater's presence in Iraq being illegal under the 1989 UN Mercenary Convention, the United States had not signed the resolution. The company was operating without a license, although it claimed that it worked *for* the State Department and CIA, meaning it was not required to possess one.[193] A month after the killing, the United States Congress passed a bill that subjected all private contractors to the Military Extraterritorial Jurisdiction Act and thus subject to prosecution by United States courts.[194] In the four years and seven months prior to this amendment private companies had effectively operated with immunity from prosecution. "Private security forces faced no legal consequences for their deadly actions… they seldom faced any public outcry from Iraqi officials. Within the Bush administration they were either praised or unmentioned."[195] As author Naomi Wolf says,

[190] Scahill, J (2007). *Blackwater*. 2nd ed. London: Perseus Books Group. Pg. 20
[191] Coalition Provisional Authority. 2003. *Coalition Provisional Authority Order Number 17*. [ONLINE] Available at: www.iraqcoalition.org/regulations/20040627_CPAORD_17_Status_of_Coalition__Rev__with_Annex_A.pdf. [Accessed 03 December 11].
[192] Klein, N (2004) 'Baghdad Year Zero'. *Harper's Magazine*. September, 2004. Pg. 48
[193] Weinberger, S. (2007). *Blackwater: Banned in Iraq?*. Available: http://www.wired.com/dangerroom/2007/09/blackwater-bann/. Last accessed 4th Jan 2012.
[194] Fox News. (2007). *House Passes Bill That Would Hike Penalties for U.S. Security Contractors in Iraq*. Available: http://www.foxnews.com/story/0,2933,299370,00.html. Last accessed 3rd Dec 2011.
[195] Scahill, J (2007). *Blackwater*. 2nd ed. London: Perseus Books Group. Pg. 9

"when the FBI tried to investigate [the Blackwater controversies] the State Department blocked the investigation… when the state starts to protect its own murderers a very dangerous corner has been turned."[196] The consequences of these policies were most obvious in Abu Ghraib prison.

In 2004 CBS Broadcasting aired a television program that exposed human rights violations that had occurred at Abu Ghraib prison, a facility constructed by British contractors in the 1950s, situated in a city west of Baghdad. According to Peter Singer, "the U.S. Army found that private contractors were involved in 36% of the documented abuse incidents."[197] An interrogator from CACI International Inc. and a translator from Titan Corporation[198] had allegedly been involved in the torture and abuse of detainees.[199] No individual from either company has been prosecuted for involvement[200] because of the sovereign immunity they received from the government.[201]

3.4 Beyond the Military-Industrial Complex

In 1961 Dwight Eisenhower spoke of the expanding military department and growing arms industry as a necessary but dangerous development following the Second World War. He warned that "we must not fail to comprehend its grave implications"[202] as there was a new found potential for the disastrous rise of misplaced power. Klein terms the process surrounding the 'War on Terror' a 'disaster capitalism complex' with "much farther-reaching tentacles than the military-industrial complex that Dwight Eisenhower warned against… the ultimate goal for the corporations at the center of the complex is to bring the model of for-profit government… into the ordinary and day-to-day functioning of the state – in effect, to privatize the government."[203] John Perkins describes the concept as "a symbiotic relationship developed between governments, corporations, and multilateral organizations."[204]

It will never be clear whether information that led to the Iraq War was deliberately manipulated, or whether a series of errors meant erroneous intelligence was adopted as factual, but the war has certainly been profitable for a close-knit group of individuals. A report by the Center for Public Integrity revealed that the largest contracts the United States issued "went to companies

[196] *The End of America*, 2008. [DVD] Ricki Stern, Anne Sundberg, USA: Impact Partners.
[197] *Force Provision*, 2007. [DVD] Allie Tyler, USA: Cold Pressed Films.
[198] Titan Corporation was acquired by L-3 Communications in 2005.
[199] Scahill, J (2007). *Blackwater*. 2nd ed. London: Perseus Books Group. Pg. 221
[200] London, J. (2011). *CACI in Iraq - FAQs and Special Information.* Available: http://www.caci.com/iraq/iraq_news.shtml. Last accessed 15th July 2011.
[201] *Force Provision*, 2007. [DVD] Allie Tyler, USA: Cold Pressed Films.
[202] Eisenhower, D. (2011). *Farewell Address January 17, 1961.* Available: http://www.eisenhowermemorial.org/pages.php?pid=696. Last accessed 30th May 2011.
[203] Klein, N (2008). *The Shock Doctrine*. 2nd ed. London: Penguin Group. Pg. 12
[204] Perkins, J (2005). *Confessions of an Economic Hit Man*. London: Ebury Press. Pg. 19

that employed former high-ranking government officials, or executives with close ties to members of Congress and even the agencies awarding their contracts."[205] USAID claims the allocation of contracts were not politically motivated, but for the $49 million private companies had given in political donations at least $8 billion had been awarded to them in the form of contracts.[206] The Bush administration's policies on Iraq were those envisioned by Rumsfeld when he spoke of outsourcing the Pentagon. Policy decreed by Rumsfeld-appointed Lewis Paul Bremer created an environment where companies could invest quickly and easily in a brand new marketplace so that by 2011 there were more private contractors in the country than uniformed military personnel.[207] Confusion surrounded their legal status. They were able to monopolise enormous contracts issued by the US government, import labour, export profits and were under no obligation to serve the interests of the Iraqi people. Little or no oversight, in conjunction with contracts that secured profits, meant companies could abuse the system. One example of the exploitation was Halliburton/KBR renting the entirety of Khalifa Tourist Resort in Kuwait to house its senior staff, a complex that contained swimming pools, restaurants and its own private beach, at a cost to the taxpayer of $1.5 million a month.[208] Melissa Rossi describes the federal government behaviour towards Halliburton as 'masochistic', continually rewarding a company that persistently defrauded them.[209] The consequence of the contracts was companies from around the world and in every industry being accused of overcharging, committing human rights violations, failing to complete contracts and damaging the reputation of the military forces on the ground.

According to the Inspector General of Iraq, millions of taxpayer dollars have been wasted due to "incomplete, terminated and abandoned" projects in Iraq.[210] That money could have been better allocated towards efforts that would have provided food, clean water and security to the Iraqi people, quelling those who opposed the US-led Coalition and built an infrastructure that would have lead to a new lease of life for an Iraq plagued by oppression, sanctions and war. In 2011 a

---

[205] CBS News. (2009). *Big Contracts Went To Big Donors.* Available: http://www.cbsnews.com/stories/2003/10/30/iraq/main580998.shtml. Last accessed 12th Jul 2011.

[206] BBC News. (2003). *Iraq Contracts 'Won by Bush Donors'.* Available: http://news.bbc.co.uk/1/hi/business/3231345.stm. Last accessed 3rd Dec 2011.

[207] Congressional Research Service, 2011, Department of Defense Contractors in Afghanistan and Iraq: Background and Analysis. [pdf] Washington: Congressional Research Service. Available at: www.fas.org/sgp/crs/natsec/R40764.pdf. [Accessed 30 May 2011].

[208] Chatterjee, P (2009). *Halliburton's Army.* New York: Nation Books. Pg. 111

[209] Rossi, M (2009). *What Every American Should Know about Who's Really Running the World.* New York: Nation Books. Pg. 257

[210] Ferguson, B. (2008). *Private contractors Steal Billions From Uncle Sam.* Available: http://archive.arabnews.com/?page=4&section=0&article=112255&d=30&m=7&y=2008. Last accessed 21st, July 2011.

report by the independent bipartisan Commission on Wartime Contracting estimated that "at least $31 billion, and possibly as much as $60 billion, has been lost to contract waste and fraud in America's contingency operations in Iraq and Afghanistan."[211] The report cited the poor planning and lack of oversight taking place on projects as well as criminal behaviour as reasons for the wasted funds, warning, "lives will be lost because of waste and mismanagement."[212] These companies were also able to operate with little or no accountability. Up until 2009 contractors had been protected with total immunity from prosecution[213] until a US-Iraqi agreement altered the law. The first trial took place seven years after the initial invasion, charging an employee of security firm ArmorGroup with the killing of two colleagues. Before this no major contractor had faced legal proceedings for events they were involved in.[214]

The military-industrial complex has been realised in Iraq. The revolving door of politics meant that corporate interests played a substantial role in the planning, engaging and operating of war. With controversial evidence and against overwhelming public outcry, the conflict went ahead. Financial benefits have only been realised for a small group of companies that secured contracts, many with links to the policy makers who legislated for the war. The true cost of the war has been seen in the deaths of thousands of military soldiers, foreign workers and local Iraqis. Those who could not survive under the new government, and opposed foreign occupation of their land, turned to violent rebellion. They were the masses the US-led occupation had left unemployed, unable to find work with the foreign contractors and not receiving the services they desperately needed.

Rumsfeld may have been sincere in his belief that outsourcing the Pentagon would eradicate bureaucracy, reduce costs and increase efficiency but the result has been the privatisation of government. Where contractors outnumbered soldiers, the war was not fought by agents of the state but by employees of conglomerates.

Warfare now not only benefits a minority of weapons producers but generates enormous revenues for companies who provide everything from the training of bodyguards to the supply of toilet paper. "These wars show no signs of being ended, let alone won. But to the defence lobby what matters is the money. It sustains combat by constantly promising success and

---

[211] Commission on Wartime Contracting in Iraq and Afghanistan. (2011). *Final Report to Congress August 2011: Transforming Wartime Contracting.* Available: www.wartimecontracting.gov/docs/CWC_FinalReport-highres.pdf. Pg. 1. Last accessed 3rd Sep 2011.
[212] *Ibid.*
[213] Wolf, N. (2007). *Fascist America, in 10 easy steps.* Available: http://www.guardian.co.uk/world/2007/apr/24/usa.comment. Last accessed 12th July 2011.
[214] Davies, C. (2010). *Briton Goes on Trial in Iraq Charged With Killing Two Colleagues.* Available: http://www.guardian.co.uk/world/2010/dec/29/british-security-contractor-iraq-trial. Last accessed 12th Jul 2011.

inducing politicians and journalists to see 'more enemy dead', 'a glimmer of hope' and 'a corner about to be turned'.[215] For the companies benefitting from the prolonged warfare their interest is in the war continuing further, the military issuing more contracts and the goods and services they provide being in ever higher demand. "Our global culture is a monstrous machine that requires exponentially increasing amounts of fuel and maintenance, so much so that in the end it will have consumed everything in sight and be left with no choice but to devour itself."[216]

Bibliography

Tariq Ali (2003). *Bush in Babylon: The Recolonisation of Iraq*. London: Verso.

---

[215] Jenkins, S. (2011). *Eisenhower's Worst Fears Came True. We Invent Enemies to Buy the Bombs.* Available: http://www.guardian.co.uk/commentisfree/2011/jun/16/eisenhower-fears-invent-enemies-buy-bombs. Last accessed 12th July 2011.
[216] Perkins, J (2005). *Confessions of an Economic Hit Man*. London: Ebury Press. Pg. xiii

Stephen Armstrong (2009). *War plc: The Rise of the New Corporate Mercenary*. 2nd ed. London: Faber and Faber Ltd.

James Ashcroft (2007). *Making A Killing: The Explosive Story of a Hired Gun in Iraq*. 2nd ed. London: Virgin Books Ltd.

James A. Baker et al (2006). *The Iraq Study Group Report: The Way Forward - a New Approach*. New York: Random House Inc.

Raymond Baker, Shereen Ismael and Tareq Ismael (2010). *Cultural Cleansing in Iraq: Why Museums Were Looted, Libraries Burned and Academics Murdered*. New York: Pluto Press.

Scott Bartz (2011). *The Tylenol Mafia: Marketing, Murder, and Johnson & Johnson*. New York: New Light Publishing.

Emma Bircham and John Charlton (2001). *Anti-Capitalism: A Guide to the Movement*. 2nd ed. Sydney: Bath Press.

Hans Blix (2005). *Disarming Iraq: The Search for Weapons of Mass Destruction*. London: Bloomsbury Publishing Plc.

Dan Briody (2004). *The Halliburton Agenda: The Politics of Oil and Money*. New Jersey: John Wiley & Sons Inc.

Dan Briody (2004). *The Iron Triangle: Inside the Secret World of The Carlyle Group*. New Jersey: John Wiley & Sons.

Vincent Bugliosi (2008). *The Prosecution of George W. Bush for Murder*. London: Perseus Book Group.

Smedley D. Butler (2003). *War is a Racket*. 2nd ed. Los Angeles: Feral House.

Rajiv Chandrasekaran (2008). *Imperial Life in the Emerald City: Inside Baghdad's Green Zone*. 2nd ed. London: Bloomsbury Publishing Plc.

Pratap Chatterjee (2009). *Halliburton's Army: How a Well-Connected Texas Oil Company Revolutionized the Way America Makes War*. New York: Nation Books.

Pratap Chatterjee (2004). *Iraq, Inc.: A Profitable Occupation*. Toronto: Seven Stories Press.

Noam Chomsky (2004). *Hegemony or Survival: America's Quest for Global Dominance*. 3rd ed. London: Penguin Group.

Tom Devine; Tarek Maassarani (2011). *The Corporate Whistleblower's Survival Guide*. California: Berrett-Koehler Publishers Inc.

Lou Dubose and Jake Bernstein (2006). *Vice: Dick Cheney and the Hijacking of the American Presidency*. New York: Random House Publishing Group.

Benjamin Franklin (1972). *An Historical Review of the Constitution and Government of Pennsylvania*. London: Arno Press.

Milton Friedman (1972). *Capitalism and Freedom*. 12th ed. Chicago: The University of Chicago Press.

James Fulcher (2004). *Capitalism: A Very Short Introduction*. New York: Oxford University Press.

Nicholas Gilby (2009). *The No-Nonsense Guide to the Arms Trade*. 2nd ed. Oxford: New Internationalist Publications Ltd.

William Hartung (2011). *Prophets of War: Lockheed Martin and the Making of the Military-Industrial Complex*. New York: Nation Books.

Friedrich Hayek (1997). *The Road to Serfdom*. 3rd ed. London: Routledge & Kegan Paul Ltd.

Eric Hobsbawm (2008). *Globalisation, Democracy and Terrorism*. 2nd ed. London: Little, Brown Book Group.

Ted Honderich (2006). *Right and Wrong, and Palestine, 9-11, Iraq, 7-7...*. Toronto: Seven Stories Press.

Molly Ivins; Lou Dubose (2004). *Bushwhacked: Life in George W. Bush's America*. London: Allison & Busby Limited.

Antonia Juhasz (2006). *The Bush Agenda: Invading the World, One Economy at a Time*. New York: HarperCollins Publishers Inc.

Russ Kick (2004). *50 Things You're Not Supposed to Know: Volume 2*. New York: The Disinformation Company Ltd.

Naomi Klein (2008). *The Shock Doctrine: The Rise of Disaster Capitalism*. 2nd ed. London: Penguin Group.

Gérard Kreijen (2004). *State Failure, Sovereignty and Effectiveness*. Oegstgeest: Brill Academic Publishers.

Michael Lee Lanning (2005). *Mercenaries*. New York: Random House Inc.

Niccolò Machiavelli (1993). *Machiavelli: The Prince*. 5th ed. Cambridge: Cambridge University Press.

David Miller (2003). *Political Philosophy: A Very Short Introduction*. New York: Oxford University Press.

Mark Crispin Miller (2005). *Cruel and Unusual: Bush/Cheney's New World Order*. New York: W. W. Norton & Company, Inc.

Michael Moore (2003). *Dude, Where's My Country?*. London: Penguin Group.

Michael Moore (2004). *The Official Fahrenheit 9/11 Reader*. New York: Simon & Schuster Inc.

The National Commission on Terrorist Attacks Upon the United States (2004). *The 9/11 Commission Report*. New York: W. W. Norton & Company Ltd.

Richard Osborne (1992). *Philosophy for Beginners*. London: Zidane Press.

Greg Palast (2004). *The Best Democracy Money Can Buy: An Investigative Reporter Exposes the Truth About Globalization, Corporate Cons and High Finance Fraudsters*. 2nd ed. London: Plume Books.

Ron Paul (2011). *Liberty Defined: 50 Essential Issues That Affect Our Freedom*. New York: Grand Central Publishing.

John Perkins (2005). *Confessions of an Economic Hit Man*. London: Ebury Press. Pg. xiii

John Pilger (2002). *The New Rulers of the World*. London: New Left Books.

William Polk (2005). *Understanding Iraq: The Whole Sweep of Iraqi History, from Genghis Khan's Mongols to the Ottoman Turks to the British Mandate to the American Occupation*. London: I.B.Tauris & Co Ltd.

John Prados (2004). *Hoodwinked: How the Bush Administration Sold Us a War*. New York: The New Press.

Thomas Ricks (2007). *Fiasco: The American Military Adventure in Iraq*. London: Penguin Group.

Melissa Rossi (2009). *What Every American Should Know about Who's Really Running the World*. New York: Nation Books.

Bertrand Russell (1963). *Political Ideals*. London: George Allen & Unwin Publishers Ltd.

Jeremy Scahill (2007). *Blackwater: The Rise of the World's Most Powerful Mercenary Army*. 2nd ed. London: Perseus Books Group.

Second Continental Congress (2008). *The Constitution of the United States of America with the Bill of Rights and all of the Amendments*. Virginia: Wilder Publications.

Peter Singer (2008). *Corporate Warriors: The Rise of the Privatized Military Industry*. 2nd ed. New York: Cornell University Press.

Joseph Stiglitz and Linda Bilmes (2008). *The Three Trillion Dollar War: The True Cost of the Iraq Conflict*. London: Penguin Group.

Peter Stone and Joanne Bajjaly (2008). *The Destruction of Cultural Heritage in Iraq*. Suffolk: The Bodywell Press.

Ron Suskind (2007). *The One Percent Doctrine: Deep Inside America's Pursuit of Its Enemies Since 9/11*. 2nd ed. London: Pocket Books.

Sun Tzu (2010). *The Art of War*. London: Arcturus Publishing Limited.

Craig Unger (2004). *House of Bush House of Saud: The Secret Relationship Between the World's Two Most Powerful Dynasties*. New York: Gibson Square Books Ltd.

Gore Vidal (2003). *Dreaming War: Blood for Oil and the Cheney-Bush Junta*. Wiltshire: Cromwell Press Limited.

David Vine (2011). *Island of Shame: The Secret History of the U.S. Military Base on Diego Garcia*. 4th ed. New Jersey: Princeton University Press.

Bob Woodward (2004). *Plan of Attack*. New York: Simon & Schuster Inc.

Newspapers and Magazines

Forbes. December 8th 2003.

Harper's Magazine. September 2004.

The Wall Street Journal. 28th April 2004.

The Wall Street Journal. 17th December 2007.

The Wall Street Journal. 2nd February 2003.

Journals

Annual Mortality Rates and Excess Deaths of Children under Five in Iraq, 1991-98. (2003). *Population Studies*.

Military-Advisory Groups and African Security: Privatised Peacekeeping. *International Peacekeeping*, Vol. 5, No. 3 (Autumn 1998).

Stephen Zunes. 'An Annotated Overview of the Foreign Policy Segments of President George W. Bush's State of the Union Address,' *Foreign Policy in Focus*, January 29, 2003.

Webography

Al Jazeera. http://www.aljazeera.com/

American Business Journals. http://www.bizjournals.com/

Arab News. http://www.arabnews.com/

BBC News. http://news.bbc.co.uk/

Berfrois. http://www.berfrois.com/

Bloomberg L.P. http://www.bloomberg.com/

Cable News Network. http://www.cnn.com/

CACI International Inc. http://www.caci.com/

The Cato Institute. http://www.cato.org/

CBS News. http://www.cbsnews.com/

The Center for Public Integrity. http://projects.publicintegrity.org/

The Center for Public Integrity iWatch News. http://http://www.iwatchnews.org/

Center for Responsive Politics. http://www.opensecrets.org/

Coalition Provisional Authority. http://www.iraqcoalition.org/

Commission on Wartime Contracting. http://www.wartimecontracting.gov/

Common Dreams NewsCenter. http://www.commondreams.org/

The Commonwealth Institute. http://www.comw.org/

CorpWatch. http://www.corpwatch.org/

Dwight D. Eisenhower Memorial Commission. http://www.eisenhowermemorial.org/

Federation of American Scientists. http://www.fas.org/

Fox News Channel. http://www.foxnews.com/

Government Executive. http://www.govexec.com/

The Guardian. http://www.guardian.co.uk/

Halliburton Company. http://www.halliburton.com/

Halliburton Watch. http://www.halliburtonwatch.org/

The Independent. http://www.independent.co.uk/

Iraq Body Count. http://www.iraqbodycount.org/

Iraq Coalition Casualty Count. http://www.icasualties.org/

Los Angeles Times. http://www.latimes.com/

Massachusetts Institute of Technology. ocw.mit.edu/

Mother Jones. http://motherjones.com/

The New American. http://www.thenewamerican.com/

The New York Times. http://www.nytimes.com/

Overseas Civilian Contractors. civiliancontractors.wordpress.com/

Philadelphia City Paper. http://www.citypaper.net/

Press Release Distribution. http://www.prlog.org/

Project Vote Smart. http://www.votesmart.org/

United States Department of Defense. http://www.defense.gov/

United States Department of State. http://fpc.state.gov/

Project Vote Smart. http://www.votesmart.org/

The Washington Post. http://www.washingtonpost.com/

Filmography

The End of America. (2008) [DVD] Ricki Stern, Anne Sundberg, USA: Impact Partners.

Fahrenheit 9/11. (2004) [DVD] United States: Dog Eat Dog Films, Miramax Films.

Force Provision. (2007) [DVD] Allie Tyler, USA: Cold Pressed Films.

Iraq for Sale: The War Profiteers. (2006) [DVD] United States: Brave New Films.

Iraq in Fragments. (2006) [DVD] United States: Daylight Factory, Typecast Pictures.

No End in Sight: Iraq's Descent into Chaos. (2007) [DVD] United States: Red Envelope Entertainment, Representational Pictures.

Shadow Company. (2006) [DVD] Nick Bicanic, Jason Bourque, Canada: Purpose Films.

The Oil Factor: Behind the War on Terror. (2005) [DVD] Audrey Brohy, USA: Free-Will Productions.

Taxi to the Dark Side. (2007) [DVD] United States: Jigsaw Productions.

Uncovered: The War on Iraq. (2004) [DVD] Robert Greenwald, USA: Cinema Libre Studio.

War Made Easy. (2008) [DVD] Jeremy Earp, Loretta Alper, USA: Media Education Foundation.

Why We Fight. (2005) [DVD] Eugene Jarecki, USA: Arte Films.